D1709561

Great Artists

Georgia O'Keeffe

ABDO
Publishing Company

Joanne Mattern

visit us at
www.abdopub.com

Published by ABDO Publishing Company, 4940 Viking Drive, Edina, Minnesota 55435.
Copyright © 2005 by Abdo Consulting Group, Inc. International copyrights reserved in all
countries. No part of this book may be reproduced in any form without written permission from
the publisher. The Checkerboard Library™ is a trademark and logo of ABDO Publishing
Company.

Printed in the United States.

Cover Photo: Getty Images
Interior Photos: Corbis pp. 9, 11, 17, 23, 25, 29; Getty Images pp. 1, 5, 13, 15, 19, 21, 27

Series Coordinator: Megan Murphy
Editors: Heidi M. Dahmes, Stephanie Hedlund
Cover Design: Neil Klinepier
Interior Design: Dave Bullen

Library of Congress Cataloging-in-Publication Data

Mattern, Joanne, 1963-
      Georgia O'Keeffe / Joanne Mattern.
         p. cm. -- (Great artists)
      Includes index.
      ISBN 1-59197-846-7
      1. O'Keeffe, Georgia, 1887-1986--Juvenile literature. 2. Painters--United States--Biography--
Juvenile literature. I. Title.

ND237.O5M38 2005
759.13--dc22
[B]

                                                                                    2004052808

Contents

Georgia O'Keeffe

Georgia O'Keeffe is one of America's most famous artists. O'Keeffe spent many years living in New Mexico. She loved nature and was inspired by her earthy subjects. Her paintings are simple, bold, and beautiful.

At the time O'Keeffe painted, most famous artists were men. She changed the way people thought about women painters. Her unusual pictures changed the way they thought about art, too.

O'Keeffe was part of a group called modern artists. Modern artists expressed their feelings through shapes and colors. They did not always paint realistic pictures of people or places. Instead, their work was **abstract**.

Many people thought O'Keeffe was stubborn. Work was one of the most important things to her. In fact, she spent almost all of her life creating art. O'Keeffe's paintings are still a wonder to look at.

O'Keeffe poured her emotions into all of her works. She painted the world as she saw it.

Timeline

1887 ~ On November 15, Georgia Totto O'Keeffe was born near Sun Prairie, Wisconsin.

1912 ~ O'Keeffe began teaching art in Amarillo, Texas.

1915 ~ O'Keeffe created a series of charcoal drawings that later caught the attention of Alfred Stieglitz.

1924 ~ Stieglitz and O'Keeffe were married.

1925 ~ O'Keeffe painted *New York with Moon*.

1929 ~ O'Keeffe's summer trip to New Mexico inspired her own abstract style. From that time on, she spent her summers in New Mexico.

1946 ~ Stieglitz died.

1949 ~ O'Keeffe permanently moved to New Mexico.

1976 ~ O'Keeffe's autobiography was published.

1986 ~ O'Keeffe died in New Mexico on March 6.

Fun Facts

- Georgia O'Keeffe knew in eighth grade that she wanted to be an artist. She didn't remember how she came to this idea. But, she did remember that when she saw the painting *Maid of Athens*, it started an urge in her to paint.

- The O'Keeffe family had the first telephone in Sun Prairie, Wisconsin.

- In 1997, the Georgia O'Keeffe Museum opened in Santa Fe, New Mexico. It has the largest collection of her works.

- O'Keeffe always noticed the way things looked. She loved to look at light and colors. One of her earliest memories was of lying outside on a patchwork quilt. Years later, she still remembered the colors and sunlight. She distinctly remembered the brightness that surrounded her.

Farm Life

Georgia Totto O'Keeffe was born on November 15, 1887. She grew up near Sun Prairie, Wisconsin. Georgia was the second of Frank and Ida O'Keeffe's seven children.

Georgia's parents were farmers. Her father's family had come to America from Ireland about 40 years before Georgia was born. Ida was the daughter of a **count** from Hungary.

Life on the farm was full of hard work. Georgia and her sisters had chores to do, such as sewing and cooking. Georgia's brothers helped Frank with the farmwork. All of the children took care of the vegetable garden, too.

Georgia spent a lot of time outside on the family farm. And, she loved playing with her dolls. She made them clothes and a house.

Georgia loved music, too. Her mother played the piano. Many evenings, the family sang together. When she was older, Georgia did a series of works based on music.

O'Keeffe's art was often influenced by her childhood on a farm. She painted Red Barn in Wheatfield *in 1928.*

School Days

Education was important to Georgia's mother. So, Georgia started school just before her fifth birthday. She went to a one-room schoolhouse for seven years.

From the time Georgia was nine years old, the three oldest O'Keeffe girls had taken art lessons in Sun Prairie. Every Saturday they learned to copy pictures by accomplished artists.

In the art lessons, Georgia copied pictures someone else had drawn. But when she got home, Georgia created her own pictures. She painted places she had only seen in books. She painted a lighthouse, the sea, and palm trees.

When she was 12 years old, Georgia left the local school because it wasn't challenging enough. She then attended a **convent** school in Madison, Wisconsin. There, Georgia had classes in art and classical music.

O'Keeffe may have attended a one-room schoolhouse similar to this one. Many small settlements in the 1800s and early 1900s had this type of school.

Down South

In 1902, Georgia and her brother Francis moved to Milwaukee, Wisconsin. They lived with an aunt and went to the public high school. That winter, the O'Keeffes decided to move to Williamsburg, Virginia.

The next summer, Georgia moved to Virginia to be with her family. She found that life in the south was very different than it was in Wisconsin.

In Wisconsin, Georgia wore practical clothes and worked as hard as her brothers. But in Virginia, the girls Georgia met wore pretty dresses. They did not do hard physical work.

Georgia went to a boarding school called the Chatham Episcopal Institute. She was different from the other girls. She wore plain clothes and pulled her hair back into a simple braid.

When the girls got to know Georgia, they liked her a lot. She was funny and smart. And, she liked to have a good time. She even taught the girls how to play poker!

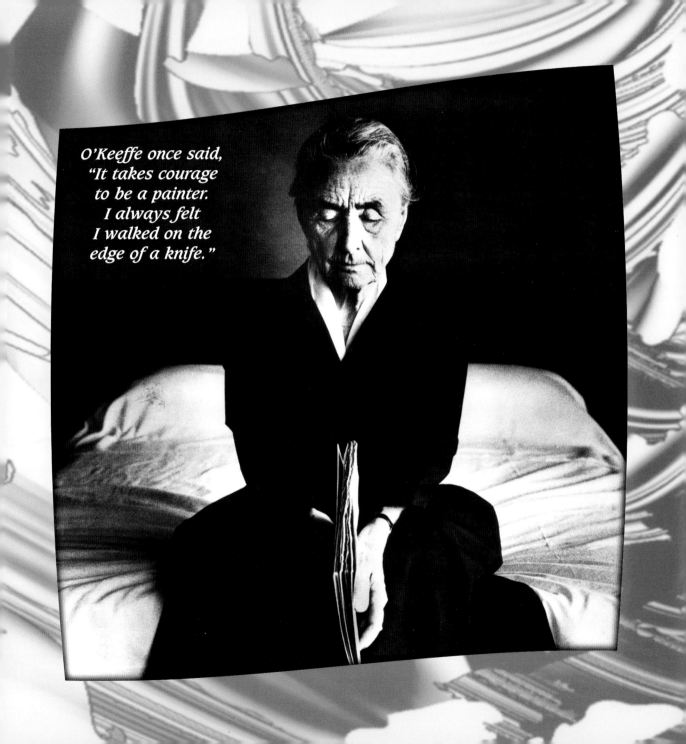

O'Keeffe once said, "It takes courage to be a painter. I always felt I walked on the edge of a knife."

Art Lessons

When Georgia graduated from Chatham, she told her classmates, "I am going to give up everything for my art." The first thing she gave up was her home. Georgia traveled to Chicago, Illinois, to attend the Art Institute.

The Art Institute of Chicago was very traditional. The school focused on European artists. So, teachers often had students copy European paintings. Georgia took figure-drawing classes, which did not interest her.

Despite her dislike for copying art and drawing people, Georgia persisted in her studies. At the end of the year, her professor ranked her first in her class.

From 1907 to 1908, Georgia studied at the Art Students League of New York. She learned many things at this school. Georgia learned how to paint **still lifes**. She also studied ways to make a flat canvas look **three-dimensional**.

The Art Institute of Chicago

Unlike the Art Institute of Chicago, the Art Students League encouraged individuality. When the term ended, one of Georgia's **still lifes** won her a **scholarship**. She earned a trip to a retreat for artists in upstate New York.

New Approach

O'Keeffe loved her exciting life in New York City. But, she was only able to stay for a year. Her father had started a concrete-making business. When the business failed, there was no money to pay for O'Keeffe's classes at the Art Students League. So, she quit her studies and started earning money.

In the fall of 1908, O'Keeffe moved back to Chicago. She worked as a **freelance** illustrator for advertising agencies. The work was hard and boring.

While working as a freelancer, O'Keeffe got a bad case of the **measles**. The disease affected her eyes, and for a while she could not see well enough to draw. She quit working and went home to Virginia.

In 1912, O'Keeffe was well enough to begin taking art classes at the University of Virginia. Her teacher, Alon Bement, taught Arthur Wesley Dow's ideas. Dow believed that the goal of an artist was personal expression of ideas and feelings.

Bement showed O'Keeffe how simple **composition** created a powerful painting. The ideas of Dow and Bement helped O'Keeffe take a new approach to her own art. One of her earliest **watercolors** using Dow's ideas is *Tent Door at Night*.

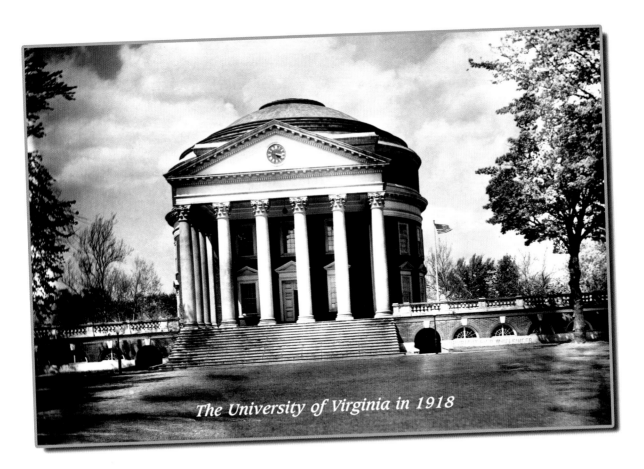

The University of Virginia in 1918

Wild West

In 1912, O'Keeffe took a job as an art teacher at a public school in Amarillo, Texas. She had read about the Western landscape in books. She was very excited to go to the Wild West where Billy the Kid had been.

O'Keeffe loved Texas. For the first time, she lived in the desert. She thought the West was a wild, beautiful place. And she loved the wind, dust, and sun.

O'Keeffe was a talented and popular teacher. For the next two years, she taught in Amarillo during the school year. During the summers, she worked at the University of Virginia.

O'Keeffe enjoyed teaching, but she needed a change. So in 1914, she went back to New York to study at Columbia University's Teachers College. O'Keeffe also spent a lot of time at photographer Alfred Stieglitz's art gallery 291.

Stieglitz and O'Keeffe had met a few years earlier at the Art Students League. Stieglitz liked a new style of art called modern art. Many people thought modern art was ugly. But O'Keeffe liked it. She also admired the way Stieglitz stood up for what he believed in.

Modern Eye

Alfred Stieglitz was born on January 1, 1864, in Hoboken, New Jersey. His family moved to Europe in 1881. While studying at the Berlin Polytechnic in 1883, Stieglitz discovered photochemistry.

Stieglitz moved to the United States in 1890. In 1902, he founded the Photo-Secession Group. In 1905, the group started their own gallery, known as 291. Stieglitz was a supporter of modern art. And, he is responsible for bringing recognition to many contemporary American artists.

Some of Stieglitz's most famous photographs are a 400-print series of Georgia O'Keeffe. He is also well-known for his series of clouds that seem to convey emotions. And, he was a pioneer in taking photographs in the rain and snow and at night.

Success

In 1915, O'Keeffe was teaching art in South Carolina. She decided she wanted to develop her own style of expression. So, she created a series of **charcoal** drawings.

O'Keeffe was very excited. These pictures were unlike anything she had ever done. She sent them to her friend Anita Pollitzer. Pollitzer loved the drawings and showed them to Stieglitz on January 1, 1916.

Stieglitz was thrilled when he saw what O'Keeffe had done. He said, "Finally a woman on paper." He also said of the drawings, "They're the purest, finest sincerest things that have entered 291 in a long while . . ." Stieglitz later exhibited ten of her drawings in his gallery.

In September 1916, O'Keeffe returned to Texas to teach. Once again, the beauty of the West inspired her. O'Keeffe walked, camped, climbed, and shot guns on the wild landscape.

She even brought the skull and leg bones of cattle into her classroom to inspire her students.

O'Keeffe's artwork was not what most popular artists painted at that time. It was also unusual for a woman to be a successful artist. O'Keeffe did not care. She painted the way she wanted to.

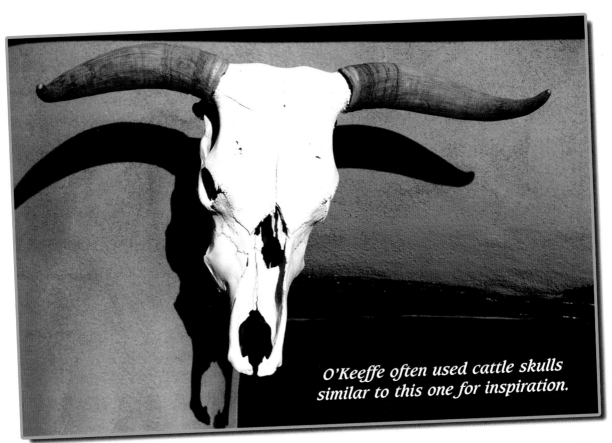

O'Keeffe often used cattle skulls similar to this one for inspiration.

Love and Art

In 1918, Stieglitz asked O'Keeffe to move back to New York City. He wanted her to paint for a year. Shortly after she arrived, the two fell in love. And in 1924, they were married.

In November 1925, the couple moved into the Shelton Hotel in New York City. That year, O'Keeffe painted the city from their suite high above the ground. Her first New York scene was called *New York with Moon*. It is a night scene of Forty-Seventh Street.

In the mid-1920s, O'Keeffe also started painting huge pictures of flowers. People were startled to see such huge, close-up pictures of small objects. O'Keeffe explained that she felt people moved too fast. They did not pay attention to little things.

O'Keeffe wanted her work to get noticed. She thought that if she painted very large flowers, people would stop and look at them. The size also shows the importance of the objects to O'Keeffe. Her large-scale flowers are some of her best-known pieces.

Artist's Corner

Georgia O'Keeffe

In the late 1920s, O'Keeffe added a new element to her already stunning art. *East River, New York No. II* displays this new method. O'Keeffe painted small objects in the front of the canvas. Behind the near objects lies a deep background. O'Keeffe cut out the middle ground.

O'Keeffe admitted that she adopted this idea from Chinese art. Chinese paintings place near and far figures on the same field with no middle ground to transition the viewer's eyes. This lack of middle ground was used in all of O'Keeffe's major series.

This Chinese drawing doesn't use middle ground.

Two Worlds

O'Keeffe was beginning to tire of New York. In 1929, she took a trip to New Mexico. As soon as she arrived, O'Keeffe felt like she had come home. This trip inspired her own **abstract** style.

In New Mexico, O'Keeffe painted many pictures. She took natural objects and showed them in new ways. O'Keeffe's paintings from this time are full of dramatic colors and shapes.

O'Keeffe's experience with photography is evident in these works. She played with space by presenting things close-up or at long range. She incorporated magnification and cropping of objects in her paintings, too. Nineteen of her New Mexico paintings were exhibited in February 1930.

When O'Keeffe returned to New York, she brought a barrel of bones with her. She was not satisfied with the paintings she had done. She needed the desert with her in the big city to keep her working.

From then on, O'Keeffe lived in two worlds. Unlike O'Keeffe, Stieglitz did not like to travel. So, O'Keeffe spent the winters in New York with Stieglitz. In the summer, she went to New Mexico by herself.

Common Subjects

O'Keeffe loved nature. In fact, she used to eat dirt as a child, which did not please her family. So, most of O'Keeffe's favorite art subjects came from the outdoors. Often enlarged views of skulls, animal bones, flowers, plants, shells, rocks, and mountains fill her canvases.

Among O'Keeffe's best-known works are her close-ups of flowers. These paintings gained her recognition as an important and successful American artist.

O'Keeffe's paintings often looked like this close-up of a flower.

Life After Alfred

Stieglitz and O'Keeffe were partners in life and in the world of art. Stieglitz was 23 years older than O'Keeffe. In 1946, Alfred Stieglitz suffered a stroke and died.

O'Keeffe spent months going through Stieglitz's photographs and other works in his collection. She helped organize two exhibitions to honor her late husband.

One show displayed Stieglitz's work. The other consisted of his art collection that he had built up over the years. The shows opened in 1947. O'Keeffe later divided his collection and **donated** portions to seven museums.

In 1949, O'Keeffe moved to New Mexico. She bought a simple adobe house. There, she created a studio out of an old stable on the Ghost Ranch property.

O'Keeffe shows Pelvis Series Red and Yellow *in 1960.*

O'Keeffe spent most of the rest of her life at Ghost Ranch. Although she had a lot of money, O'Keeffe lived simply. Her house was decorated with few objects. And, she had a large garden where she grew some of her own food.

Fascinating Life

Work was the center of O'Keeffe's life, and it thrilled her. Her commitment was an example to women. It was important to her that women make work a priority in their lives.

In her later years, O'Keeffe won many awards and honors. In 1970, she won the gold medal for painting from the National Institute of Arts and Letters.

In 1976, her **autobiography** was published. The next year, she received the Presidential Medal of Freedom. And in 1985, she received the National Medal of Arts.

O'Keeffe had begun losing her eyesight in 1971. However, she painted in oil until the mid-1970s. Then, her failing eyesight forced her to move to different **mediums**. She worked in pencil and **watercolor** until 1982. And she made pottery until 1984, when her health failed.

Georgia Totto O'Keeffe died on March 6, 1986. She was a great artist who found beauty in ordinary objects. She made flowers, buildings, and animal skulls special and exciting. O'Keeffe's art is still inspiring people today.

O'Keeffe's studio

Glossary

abstract - relating to something that doesn't represent a real object but expresses ideas or emotions.

autobiography - a story of a person's life that is written by himself or herself.

charcoal - a soft, black material that is a form of carbon.

composition - the way in which something is put together, created, or arranged.

convent - a building occupied by nuns.

count - a noble who was the governor of a county.

donate - to give.

freelance - a person who sells work to anyone who will buy it.

measles - an illness that causes a fever and rash.

medium - a mode of artistic expression or communication.

scholarship - a gift of money to help a student pay for instruction.

still life - a painting or picture made up of nonmoving objects.

three-dimensional - having the illusion of depth.

watercolor - a paint made by mixing dye with water.

Saying It

Alfred Stieglitz - AL-fruhd STEEG-luhts
Chatham - CHAT-uhm
Milwaukee - mihl-WAW-kee

Web Sites

To learn more about Georgia O'Keeffe, visit ABDO Publishing Company on the World Wide Web at **www.abdopub.com**. Web sites about O'Keeffe are featured on our Book Links page. These links are routinely monitored and updated to provide the most current information available.

Index